PLANT-TASTIC! YIKES!

POISON PLANTS

BY REX RUBY

Minneapolis, Minnesota

Credits
Cover and title page, © nikamata/iStock and © Sergii Koval/Shutterstock; 4–5, © Manfred Val-entin Ramminger/imageBROKER/Alamy; 6, © Wirestock/iStock; 6–7, © OlyaSolodenko/iStock; 8–9, © LianeM/iStock; 10L, © mcsilvey/iStock; 10R, © mariusFM77/iStock; 11, © t_kimura/iStock and © DutchScenery/iStock; 12, © I. Rottlaender/Shutterstock; 12–13, © Simon Groewe/Shutterstock; 14–15, © Chase D'animulls/Shutterstock; 16–17, © blickwin-kel/Koenig/Alamy; 18–19, © Wirestock, Inc./Alamy; 19, © Stephen Orsillo/Adobe Stock; 20–21, © leekris/Adobe Stock; 21, © Michael Moloney/Adobe Stock; 22 Step 1, © fcafotodigital/iStock and © loops7/iStock; 22 Step 2, © loops7/iStock; 22 Step 3, © Prostock-Studio/iStock; 22 Step 4, © AlexandrBognat/iStock; 22 Step 5, © djedzura/iStock; and 23, © SondraP/iStock.

Bearport Publishing Company Product Development Team
President: Jen Jenson; Director of Product Development: Spencer Brinker; Managing Editor: Allison Juda; Associate Editor: Naomi Reich; Senior Designer: Colin O'Dea; Associate Designer: Elena Klinkner; Associate Designer: Kayla Eggert; Product Development Specialist: Anita Stasson

Library of Congress Cataloging-in-Publication Data

Names: Ruby, Rex, author.
Title: Yikes! : poison plants / by Rex Ruby.
Other titles: Poison plants
Description: Minneapolis, Minnesota : Bearport Publishing Company, [2024] | Series: Plant-tastic! | Includes bibliographical references and index.
Identifiers: LCCN 2022058246 (print) | LCCN 2022058247 (ebook) | ISBN 9798888220450 (library binding) | ISBN 9798888222386 (paperback) | ISBN 9798888223604 (ebook)
Subjects: LCSH: Poisonous plants--Juvenile literature. | Dangerous plants--Juvenile literature.
Classification: LCC QK100.A1 R83 2024 (print) | LCC QK100.A1 (ebook) | DDC 581.6/59--dc23/eng/20221209
LC record available at https://lccn.loc.gov/2022058246
LC ebook record available at https://lccn.loc.gov/2022058247

Copyright © 2024 Bearport Publishing Company. All rights reserved. No part of this publication may be reproduced in whole or in part, stored in any retrieval system, or transmitted in any form or by any means, electronic, mechanical, photocopying, recording, or otherwise, without written permission from the publisher.

For more information, write to Bearport Publishing, 5357 Penn Avenue South, Minneapolis, MN 55419.

CONTENTS

Danger in the Garden 4
Don't Eat Me! 6
Wicked Wolfsbane 8
Poisonous Bulbs 10
Deadly Berries 12
Birds and Berries 14
Rosary Pea Seeds 16
A Dangerous Tree 18
Stay Away! 20

Science Lab 22
Glossary 23
Index 24
Read More 24
Learn More Online 24
About the Author 24

DANGER IN THE GARDEN

A farmer's goat has escaped from its pen. The animal is searching for something to eat when it spots some pink flowers in a nearby garden. Just as it's about to take a bite, the farmer chases the goat away. The animal was lucky. The rhododendron (*roh*-du-DEN-druhn) flowers it was about to eat are **poisonous**!

Rhododendron plants grow in many places. If animals eat them, they might get very sick or even die.

DON'T EAT ME!

Plants can't move away from hungry animals, but they can **protect** themselves in other ways. Some plants cause a **rash** when touched. Others have poisonous parts that make anything that eats them sick. If a person or other animal survives one of these **dangerous** plants, they will know to stay away in the future.

> Many poisonous plants look similar to plants that are safe to eat. This trick makes them even more dangerous.

Water hemlock has roots that look like carrots, but one bite could kill a person.

WICKED WOLFSBANE

Monkshood is one kind of dangerous plant. Every part of it is poisonous. This plant is sometimes known as wolfsbane because it was used to kill wolves a long time ago. Even a tiny amount can stop the heart of an animal as large as a fully grown wolf.

Hunters used to dip the tips of their arrows in the plant's poison to make their shots even more deadly.

POISONOUS BULBS

Sometimes, the most dangerous parts of plants are hidden from sight. Daffodils grow from round underground **bulbs**. These bulbs look a lot like onions. But if an unlucky person or animal took a bite of one, they would be chomping into something poisonous!

A daffodil bulb

An onion

A single bite of a daffodil bulb can make a person **vomit** and cause bad stomach pain.

DEADLY BERRIES

The deadly nightshade plant has some of the most dangerous fruit on Earth. Its poisonous berries may look like a sweet treat, but they can kill a person. Eat these berries and you may fall into a very deep sleep—and never wake up.

Before poison from a deadly nightshade berry kills someone, it might **blur** their vision and take away their ability to talk.

BIRDS AND BERRIES

While poisonous berries are dangerous to humans and most animals, some birds can eat them without getting sick. And that's just what the plants need! When birds swallow berries, they are also swallowing the seeds inside them. Then, they fly to other places and poop out the seeds so new plants can grow.

Pokeweed berries are safe for birds, but they can make a fully grown human very sick.

ROSARY PEA SEEDS

Rosary pea plants have beautiful red-and-black seeds, but they contain one of the deadliest poisons in the world. The seeds' hard outer shells keep the poison inside. If the covering breaks, the poison comes out. Just one broken seed has enough poison to kill someone.

Sometimes, people use rosary pea seeds as beads in jewelry.

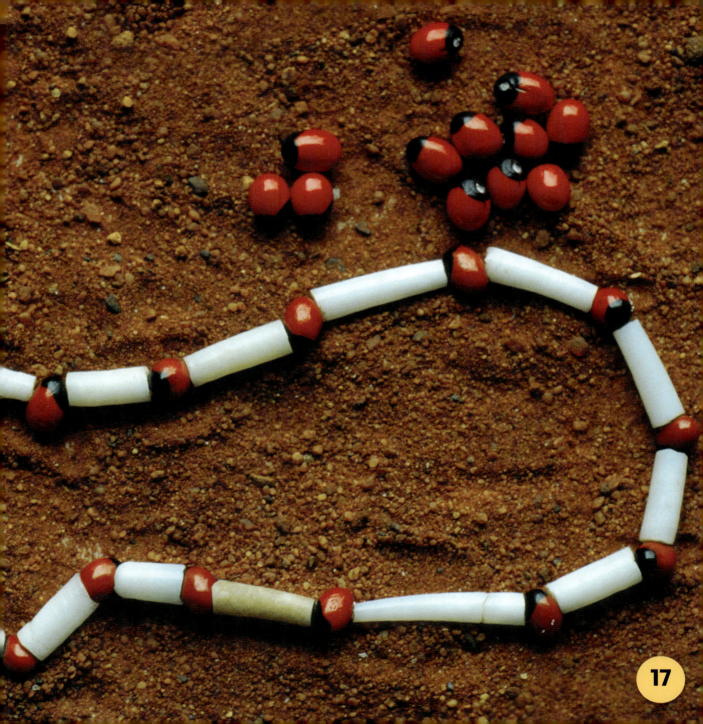

A DANGEROUS TREE

The manchineel (*man*-chuh-NEEL) tree is no ordinary plant—it's the most dangerous tree on Earth. Eating its fruit can make you very sick and may kill you. Even getting too close to this tree can be unsafe. Its leaves and branches contain a liquid that causes burns and painful **blisters** on the skin if you brush against them.

Rain that falls on manchineel trees mixes with the tree's dangerous liquid. Anyone underneath its branches has to watch out for the painful drips!

STAY AWAY!

Danger can come from anywhere—it may even be in your backyard. Touching poison ivy or poison oak plants can cause a burning rash on your skin. You can even get a rash by touching something that has brushed against these plants. Whether leaving you scratching or throwing up lunch, poisonous plants are sending a strong message: Stay away!

When mixed with sunlight, wild parsnip can create a painful rash.

Poison ivy

SCIENCE LAB
A POISON PLANT BOOK

Make a book with all you know about poisonous plants. Include your favorite plants from this book or use the internet to learn about others.

1. Staple two or more sheets of paper together along one side.

2. Make your book cover on the first piece of paper. Then, write the name of poisonous plants at the top of the other pages.

3. Research each plant.

4. Next, write a few sentences about each plant and add drawings to each page.

5. Share your book with friends and family.

GLOSSARY

blisters raised spots on the skin

blur to become unclear

bulbs the rounded, underground parts of some plants that the rest of the plant grows from

dangerous likely to cause harm or injury

poisonous having a substance that can harm or kill

protect to keep someone or something safe

rash spots or red patches on skin that are usually itchy or sore

vomit to throw up

INDEX

arrows 8
birds 14
daffodil
 bulbs 10–11
deadly nightshade
 berries 12–13
manchineel
 trees 18–19
monkshood 8
poison ivy 20–21
pokeweed berries 14
rhododendron 4–5
rosary pea seeds 16
seeds 14, 16

READ MORE

Davies, Monika. *Plants Can Poison! (Plants with Superpowers).* New York: Gareth Stevens Publishing, 2023.

Finan, Catherine C. *Plants (X-treme Facts: Science).* Minneapolis: Bearport Publishing Company, 2021.

Markovics, Joyce. *Poisonous Plants (Beware! Killer Plants).* Ann Arbor, MI: Cherry Lake Publishing, 2022.

LEARN MORE ONLINE

1. Go to **www.factsurfer.com** or scan the QR code below.
2. Enter "**Yikes**" into the search box.
3. Click on the cover of this book to see a list of websites.

ABOUT THE AUTHOR

Rex Ruby lives in Minnesota with his family. Although he tries to stay away from poisonous plants, somehow he always finds the poison ivy.